Step by Step Art for Nursery / Reception Classes

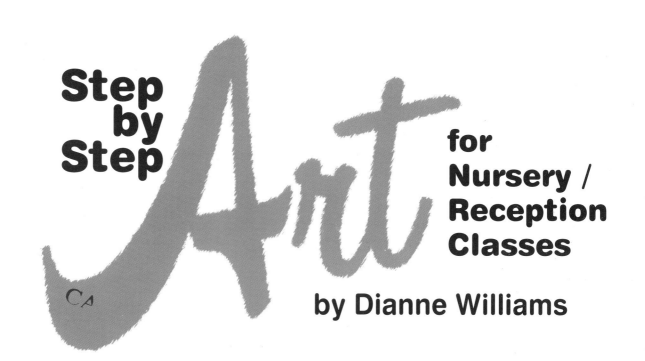

CA

by Dianne Williams

Published by
Topical Resources

Acknowledgement

The author and publisher would like to acknowledge the contribution made by the staff and pupils of the following schools during the preparation of this book. All teacher pages have been tested in the classroom. All photographed work has been produced by 4 and 5 year old children working in a classroom situation.

Astwood Bank First School, Redditch.
Beetham C.E. Primary School, Milnthorpe, Cumbria.
Castlechurch Primary School, Stafford.
Coppice Primary School, Heanor, Derbyshire.
Danesfield School, Medmenham, Bucks.
Devonshire Infant School, Smethwick.
Dosthill County Primary School, Tamworth.
Earls Barton Infants School, Northants.
Manor Way Primary School, Halesowen.

Step by Step Art is available from all good Educational Bookshops and by mail order from:

Topical Resources, P.O. Box 329, Broughton, Preston, Lancashire. PR3 5LT

Topical Resources publishes a range of Educational Materials for use in Primary Schools and Pre-School Nurseries and Playgroups.

For the latest catalogue Tel/Fax 01772 863158

Printed in Great Britain for "Topical Resources", Publishers of Educational Materials, P.O. Box 329, Broughton, Preston, Lancashire PR3 5LT (Telephone or Fax 01772 863158), by T.Snape & Company Limited, Boltons Court, Preston Lancashire.

Typeset by Paul Sealey Illustration & Design, 3 Wentworth Drive, Thornton, Lancashire.

First Published September 1997.

ISBN 1 872977 13 8

Contents

Drawing

Painting

Printing

Collage

Sculpture

Textiles

Introduction

This book is intended for teachers of young children to help them develop their 'pupils understanding and enjoyment of art, craft and design' (NC Art Orders). It will support teachers as they deliver the Early Years curriculum (Desirable Learning Outcomes) as they progress towards the National Curriculum Programme of Study.

The sessions are planned to introduce children to a wide range of tools and techniques, to encourage language and discussion and to develop skills in a sequential series of activities. The areas targeted are drawing, painting, printing, collage, textiles and sculpture which are the content of the National Curriculum Art Document. The visual elements of art i.e: language of the subject, line, tone, texture, pattern etc., are identified in relation to each session and links are made with work of other artists, craftworkers and designers, both Western and non-Western.

Each individual session and its extension activities, could be used in isolation or form part of a progressive series of six lessons that focus on one media area at a time.

The necessary art materials needed for individual sessions are listed at the top of each page and the complete range of art materials needed for a section together with the suppliers from whom they can be purchased are listed at the end of each section.

All the sessions have been tried out in schools and demonstrate the achievement of very young children using the ideas in the book. To these children and teachers, I should like to express my appreciation and thanks.

Dianne Williams

Drawing

Drawing

Session　　　One

Activity　　　Making and describing different lines.

Focus　　　Line

Equipment Needed　Paper cut to A3 or A4 size - Newsprint or Free Art 80gsm quality or grey sugar paper, Felt tip pens, thick and thin (black only), pieces of string, ribbon, or a skipping rope.

Talk About
- The lines that can be made with a piece of string/ribbon/ cord or a skipping rope on the floor.
- The lines that could be drawn in the air with a finger.
- Lines observed on objects, clothes and around the room.
- Names for a vocabulary of "line" words e.g. wriggly, slippery etc.
- Felt tip pens and how to hold them for drawing.

Doing
- Chose a thick **or** thin pen - experiment with it drawing lots of different lines
- Now draw a line that you can see somewhere in the room - point to it and describe it.
- Add more lines in the same way.
- Next draw lines that are eg. long and fat, short and wriggly etc.
- Now draw new lines of your own and talk about them.
- Finally use lots of different lines on your paper, some up and down, some from side to side to cover the page.

Developing the Idea
- Encourage the children to use both thick and thin black felt pens and to observe how each one will alter the same line.
- Allow the children to explore their vocabulary of line in colour using thick and thin coloured felt tip pens
- From individual line drawings extend the approach to a large scale group/class collaborative line collection.

Links with AT2 (Knowledge & Understanding of Other Artists)

Paul Klee

Joan Miro.

Drawing

Session	Two
Activity	Making a line that changes: (a) across a page, (b) using different drawing tools and what to call them.
Focus	Line
Equipment Needed	Paper cut to A3 or A4 size. Newsprint or Free Art 80gsm quality or grey sugar paper. (a) Felt tip pens thick or thin (black only). (b) Crayon, oil pastel, charcoal, chalk, pencil, (black and white on grey paper - black and grey on white paper).
Talk About	• A person going for a walk - along a path, up steps, down a slope etc. • Draw in the air this walk i.e. a line that changes as it moves along. (Work as a group) • Ask individual children to draw their own "line change" for members of the group to describe. • Collect together all the different tools the children are to use for drawing and name them. • As a game ask the children to choose or match tools eg. find a crayon - find another one of these etc.
Doing	• Choose one child to start a "line walk" on a large sheet of paper. Then in turn, other children add to it. • Now ask the children to draw in felt tip pen on smaller paper their own line walk. • Next ask for specific lines eg. an up/down line, a fast/slow line before asking the children to add and describe their own lines that change. • Now ask the children to choose their favourite line and draw it once in felt pen on a new sheet of paper - then ask them to draw the same line in chalk, then charcoal etc. using each type of drawing media. • Finally focus on what has happened each time, what they have drawn with, what they liked and disliked.
Developing the Idea	• Encourage the children to try the same approach i.e. using all the different drawing media with another of their lines. • Try drawing the lines in the same direction each time e.g. diagonally • Suggest the children explore the same line, same range of media with the lines drawn in different directions. • Extend this to work on a large scale.
Links with AT2 (Knowledge & Understanding of Other Artists)	Wassily Kandinsky (Abstract work only) Edvard Munch

Drawing

Session   Three

Activity   Looking for and collecting
different lines.

Focus   Line

Equipment Needed   Viewfinders (a square of card with a window cut out. Old slide mounts are ideal.)
felt tip pens(thick and thin).
Drawing pencils, A4 paper - Newsprint or Free Art 80 gsm, red cabbage, pieces of wood, shells, twigs or other objects with lines on them.

Talk About
- Specific lines in the room e.g. a long thin line. Ask the children to point to where it is.
- Ask individuals to find specific lines e.g. a zig zag line in the room, on their clothes etc.
- Focus the children on looking and describing the lines on their hands starting with the inside of their fingers.
- Feel and describe the lines on a leaf or on half a red cabbage.
- Introduce a viewfinder to look through.

Doing
- Collect together in turns the lines seen in a viewfinder on e.g. a piece of wood. Touch then draw each line on a large shared sheet of paper.
- Now look carefully again at the lines on your hand. Draw some of the lines on paper that you saw on your your fingers, then some from your palm. Cover your paper with hand lines.
- Next choose a shell, a twig, etc. and start by drawing one sort of line you see before adding others. Use your viewfinder to help.
- Cover your paper with different shell, or twig etc. lines.
- Now draw an outline shape and put your found lines in it.

Developing the Idea
- Experiment with drawing only one of your found lines using lots of different drawing media
- Try drawing one of your found lines in different colours.
- Choose one of your found lines to make stripes across your paper. Put other found lines between the stripes to make a pattern.

Links with AT2 (Knowledge & Understanding of Other Artists)   Vincent Van Gogh

Freiderich Hundertwasser

Drawing

Jodie

Session	Four
Activity	Using different lines together: (a) at random, (b) to make a pattern.
Focus	Line and Pattern.
Equipment Needed	A range of drawing media. All media to be black or white. e.g. felt pens (thick and thin), crayons, pencils, oil pastels, charcoal, chalk, paint and thick brushes. A collection of natural and man made objects e.g. shells, pebbles, feathers etc. lace, hair combs, mop heads etc. Large sheets of grey sugar paper for group work, 15 cms x 15 cms pieces of paper for individual pattern work. Pre cut small shapes (regular and irregular) of coloured sticky paper, glue, plus a collection of coloured beads, counters, yarn string or ribbon.

Talk About

- The lines that group together when a collection of yarn, string ribbon etc. is dropped on the floor - **a random pattern**.
- The different arrangement that emerges if the children then place the yarn, string ribbon, etc. in stripes - **a regular pattern**
- Look together at a collection of objects natural and man made for random and ordered patterns. Sort them into groups.
- Make random and ordered patterns with beads, counters etc.

Doing

- First copy a random pattern like the one made with dropped yarns.
- Then set out large sheets of paper to work on plus pieces of bark as stimulus.
- Work as a group but starting one at a time. Look for, touch, then draw anywhere on the paper a line from the piece of bark. Lines will be of any length and reach in any direction, meet, be next to and cross over. A **random pattern** of lines will build up covering the paper. Use paint for drawing at the end.
- Now develop the idea and difference of **regular pattern**. The children choose a pre-cut shape to stick in the centre of their own individual paper. Draw a line all the way round the shape. This is repeated with different types of line each surrounding the one before. Make sure your lines do not cross although the shape may alter slightly as it grows.

Developing the Idea

- Choose a different object and from it make your own random line pattern.
- Make a large scale collaborative regular pattern. Finally use paint.
- Encourage the children to cut or tear their own shapes for a regular pattern.
- Work in colour - a choice of 2 or 3 colours only is best to emphasise the pattern.

Links with AT2 (Knowledge & Understanding of Other Artists)

David Hockney - (Pool Paintings)

Paul Klee

Drawing

Session Five

Activity Feeling different textures - using line to describe how they feel.

Focus Line and Texture.

Equipment Needed Felt pens (thick and thin), drawing pencils, black wax crayons, photographs of animals, plants, fruit and veg. that show different textures, pieces of bark, sandpaper, velvet etc. These are resources for children to touch and describe that present different surface qualities e.g. rough, smooth, shiny etc.

Talk About
- What texture means.
- Textured objects collected from the classroom.
- Describe and sort the textures collected.
- Discuss lines in children's books and how they convey different textures. An example could be how the different materials used in the homes of the Three Little Pigs are drawn.
- The variety of textures that can be found on one object e.g. a cauliflower.
- Pictures of birds, animals, plants etc.- discuss and compare the different textures in each group.

Doing
- Explore rubbing different textures.
- Draw lines to match the marks of your rubbings.
- Describe the textures/lines which appear in both the rubbing and the drawing.
- Collect two different textures e.g. rough/smooth. Draw lines to match what you see.
- Now draw from observation e.g. a teddy bear, focusing on one texture.
- Finally draw an object e.g. a cactus in a pot, focusing on several textures.

Developing the Idea
- Make a collage of similar textures e.g. shiny things.
- Make a collage of a variety of textures.
- Make group or individual imaginary animals by using collage material of different textures or cutting different textures from magazine photographs or using different rubbings and lines of your own.

Links with AT2 (Knowledge & Understanding of Other Artists)

Albrecht Durer - Hare

Rembrandt Van Rijn - Elephant

Drawing

Session   Six

Activity   Finding different lines in a
                    picture. Matching lines.

Focus   Line, Pattern, Shape and
                    Texture.

**Equipment
Needed**   Story books with strong linear drawings. Photographs of winter trees, the built
                    environment, pylons etc. Drawings by Van Gogh. Pool paintings by David Hockney.
                    Viewfinders, felt pens and pencils, strips and squares 15cm x 15cm of Free Art 80 gsm
                    paper or newsprint.

Talk About   • The different lines used in pictures in a children's story book.
                    • What they tell you about the people/places written about.
                    • The different lines in an artist's painting or drawing.
                    • What they tell us instead of words to describe people, places etc.
                    • How different artists use lines to describe in their own way people, places etc.

Doing   • Choose a drawing by an artist for the children to work from e.g. Van Gogh. - one per
                      child.
                    • Place a viewfinder on the drawing (this is best held in place with Blu-tack) - look for
                      lines and trace with your finger.
                    • Collect one of each sort of line you have found on your strip of paper.
                    • Move your viewfinder and collect more lines and stop when your strip is full.
                    • Now look carefully at your collection and use them in a picture or pattern of your
                      own.

**Developing
the Idea**   • Display the artist's drawings, the line strips, plus the children's final work.
                    • Include line words and the name of the artist in the display.
                    • Match the lines on the strips to the artists own lines. (The children could also do this
                      as an individual activity using strings and cottons.)
                    • In the same way, use an artist whose use of line is very different.
                    • Make a class collection of lines around a large picture.

**Links with
AT2
(Knowledge &
Understanding
of Other Artists)**

Vincent Van Gogh

Pablo Picasso

Materials

Newsprint or Free Art paper 80 gsm
Black sugar paper
Grey sugar paper
Black felt tip pens (thick and thin)
Coloured felt tip pens (thick and thin)
Wax crayons
Oil pastels
Charcoal
Chalk
Drawing pencils (4B - 6B)
Paint brushes (thick and thin)
Powder paint or ready mix paint
Palettes/Inking trays
Glue
Glue spreaders

Suppliers

NES Arnold Ltd
Ludlow Hill Road
West Bridgeford
NOTTINGHAM
NG2 6HD

Pisces
Westwood Studies
West Avenue
CREWE
Cheshire
CW1 3AD

Philip & Tracey Ltd
North Way
Andover
Hampshire
SP10 5BA

Hope Education
Orb Mill
Huddersfield Road
OLDHAM
Lancashire
OL4 2ST

Yorkshire Purchasing Organisation
41 Industrial Park
WAKEFIELD
WF2 0XE

Drawing

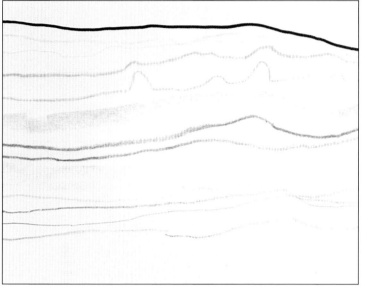

Session 2
Example of drawing a chosen line using a variety of drawing media.

Session 3
Example of repeating the same line to make a pattern.

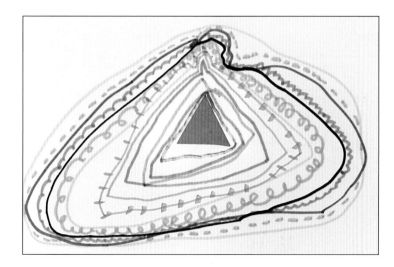

Session 4
Example of a regular pattern drawn round a shape using a variety of media.

Drawing

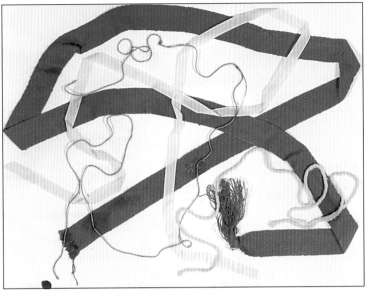

Session 4
Example of string, ribbon, yarn etc. randomly dropped and copied by a pupil using paint and felt tip pen.

Katie S.

Session 5
Example of lines drawn to match rubbings

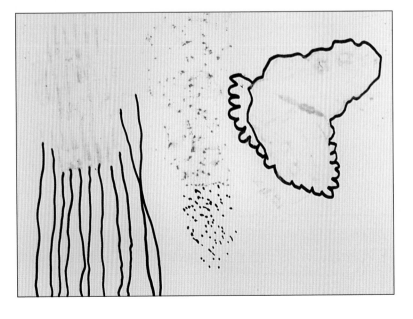

Painting

Session 1
Example of making a pattern with thick to thin marks.

Session 4
Example of filling the paper with your favourite colours.

Painting

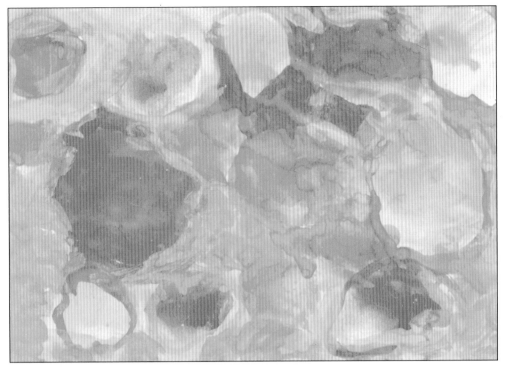

Session 5
Example of using red and yellow to make orange.

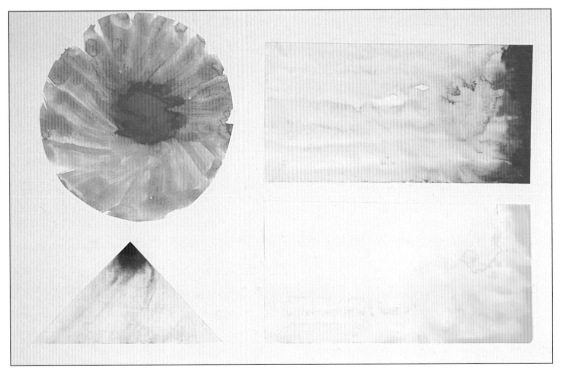

Session 6
Example of using water to make the paint paler.

Painting

Painting

Session   One

Activity   Using a thick and thin brush.

Focus   Line and Pattern.

Equipment Needed   Thick and thin brushes - one of each per child. Black ready mix or powder paint (mixed ready for use) Primary colours - red, blue, yellow for extension work. Palettes, water, paper towels. A3 or A4 sheets of white paper - Newsprint or Free Art 80 gsm. Work on a flat surface covered with newspaper.

Talk About
- Where and how to hold a brush - particularly if it has a long handle.
- Dipping the brush gently in the paint.
- Pressing firmly with a brush.
- Pressing gently with a brush.
- Describing the marks.
- How and why the same mark changes.
- Turning the paper to avoid leaning on and smudging the paint.

Doing
- First pick up a thick brush and dip it in the paint.
- Now make some thick marks by pressing the brush firmly on the paper.
- Next use the same brush but press very gently on the paper and make some thin marks.
- Now change to a thin brush. Dip it in the paint and press it firmly on the paper to make the thickest marks you can - are they as thick as the ones made with the other brush?
- Press gently with your thin brush to make thin marks - are they as thin as the ones made with the other brush?
- Finally explore making some new thick and thin marks using both brushes.

Developing the Idea
- Use your thick and thin marks to make a pattern.
- Use both brushes to make marks that start thick and end up thin.
- Use both brushes to make marks that start thin and end up thick.
- Explore making more thick to thin or thin to thick marks.
- Make a pattern with them.
- Use more than one colour of paint e.g. primary colours, red, blue, yellow.

Links with AT2 (Knowledge & Understanding of Other Artists)

Wassily Kandinsky - Landscapes

Gustav Klimt - Gardens and landscapes.

Painting

Session Two

Activity Moving paint around in different ways.

Focus Line, Shape and Texture.

Equipment Needed Thick and thin brushes. Black ready mix or powder paint (mixed ready to use). Primary colours - red, blue, yellow for extension work. Palettes, water, paper towels. A4 or A3 sheets of white paper - Newsprint or FreeArt 80 gsm. (A1 for extension work) Work on a flat surface covered with newspaper.

Talk About
- Making new marks by using a brush in different ways e.g. printing, dragging, swirling etc.
- Changing these marks by pressing gently and pressing firmly with a brush.
- Using both thick and thin brushes.
- Turning the paper to avoid leaning on and smudging the paint.

Doing
- Ask the children to choose either a thick or thin brush.
- Using a dry brush (no paint yet) suggest the children explore dabbing, swirling, dragging and stroking their brush on the paper.
- Repeat each suggestion again in turn - this time the children use black paint. Discuss the marks they have made.
- Now ask them to try the same marks using their other brush.
- Next ask them to move their brush to join some marks together and finally discover and describe new ways of using a brush.

Developing the Idea
- Explore these new marks further by pressing gently and then pressing firmly.
- Cover and fill the paper with different marks making them at random, next to, above, below, long, short, thick, thin but never crossing over (black paint only thick and thin brushes).
- Large scale - individual or group activity same ground rules/approach as above. A1 paper, thick and thin brushes plus all 3 primary colours N.B. group work requires the children to take turns when making or following a mark. Aim to fill the paper eventually!

Links with AT2 (Knowledge & Understanding of Other Artists)

Vincent Van Gogh

Gillian Ayres

Painting

Session Three

Activity Using other tools for painting.

Focus Line, Shape, Pattern, Texture.

Equipment Needed Black ready mix or powder paint. A3 or A4 paper - Newsprint or Free Art 80 gsm. Tray of twigs, lolly sticks, card, junk, etc. for painting with. Palettes, water, paper towels. Work on a flat surface covered with newspaper.

Talk About
- The different tools to paint with.
- How to hold and dip into paint.
- How to use them i.e. dab, press, drag , etc.
- Where to put the wet tools when finished with.
- Turning the paper to avoid leaning on and smudging the paint.

Doing
- Choose one new tool and dip it in the paint.
- Move it on the paper like a brush dabbing, swirling, drawing, dragging etc.
- Talk about the marks made and what the tool felt like to work with. Put the tool next to your painting.
- Now choose another tool and do the same but on another piece of paper, put the tool next to it when you have finished.
- Finally collect together and discuss groups of marks made by children using the same tools.

Developing the Idea
- Use lots of different tools to paint on the same piece of paper.
- Make a collection of thin marks using different tools.
- Make a collection of either thick, smudgy, straight, curved etc. marks using different tools.
- Make a group painting - when it is dry display next to it the tools that have been used.

Links with AT2 (Knowledge & Understanding of Other Artists) Jackson Pollock

Painting

Session   Four

Activity   Using and describing colour.

Focus   Colour and Shape.

Equipment Needed   Thick and thin brushes. A4 and A3 white paper and coloured paper. A selection of ready mix or powder paint (made up ready to use) in pots. Palettes, water, paper towels. Work on a flat surface covered with newspaper.

Talk About

- The names of the colours.
- What the colours make you think of.
- Favourite colours.
- Dull colours and bright colours.
- Using thick and thin brushes in each pot.
- Putting the brush back in the right pot when you have finished.
- Turning the paper to avoid leaning on and smudging the paint.

Doing

- Choose a piece of white paper.
- Choose one of your favourite colours.
- Paint on part of your paper.
- Change to another favourite colour.
- Paint on more of your paper.
- Continue to change colour until you have used lots of colours to fill your paper.
- Finally talk about your choice of colours and then make another painting this time using the colours you did not use before. Talk about these.

Developing the Idea

- Choose two different coloured pieces of paper.
- Put them side by side.
- Choose one paint colour to start with and fill part of each coloured piece of paper. Do your two paintings look the same?
- Now choose another paint colour and repeat on the same two pieces of paper. Look at and discuss the differences you can see.
- Add a third paint colour and discuss further.
- Work with the same three paint colours on other coloured papers to compare the effects.

Links with AT2 (Knowledge & Understanding of Other Artists)

André Derain

Claude Monet

Painting

Session   Five

Activity   Mixing colour and changing colour.

Focus   Colour

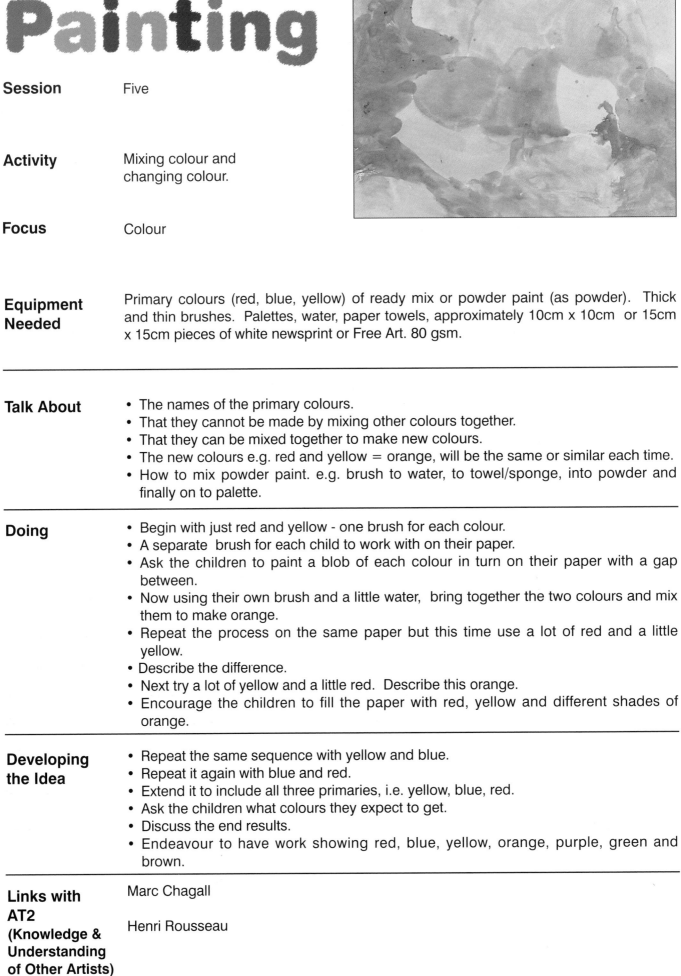

Equipment Needed   Primary colours (red, blue, yellow) of ready mix or powder paint (as powder). Thick and thin brushes. Palettes, water, paper towels, approximately 10cm x 10cm or 15cm x 15cm pieces of white newsprint or Free Art. 80 gsm.

Talk About
- The names of the primary colours.
- That they cannot be made by mixing other colours together.
- That they can be mixed together to make new colours.
- The new colours e.g. red and yellow = orange, will be the same or similar each time.
- How to mix powder paint. e.g. brush to water, to towel/sponge, into powder and finally on to palette.

Doing
- Begin with just red and yellow - one brush for each colour.
- A separate brush for each child to work with on their paper.
- Ask the children to paint a blob of each colour in turn on their paper with a gap between.
- Now using their own brush and a little water, bring together the two colours and mix them to make orange.
- Repeat the process on the same paper but this time use a lot of red and a little yellow.
- Describe the difference.
- Next try a lot of yellow and a little red. Describe this orange.
- Encourage the children to fill the paper with red, yellow and different shades of orange.

Developing the Idea
- Repeat the same sequence with yellow and blue.
- Repeat it again with blue and red.
- Extend it to include all three primaries, i.e. yellow, blue, red.
- Ask the children what colours they expect to get.
- Discuss the end results.
- Endeavour to have work showing red, blue, yellow, orange, purple, green and brown.

Links with AT2 (Knowledge & Understanding of Other Artists)   Marc Chagall

Henri Rousseau

Painting

Session	Six
Activity	More colour less colour.
Focus	Colour and Tone/Shade.
Equipment Needed	Thick and thin brushes, primary colours, (red, blue, yellow) ready mix paint or dry powder paint, water, palettes, paper towels, circles, triangles and strips or white newsprint or Free Art 80 gsm. Paint shade cards (the sort found in a D.I.Y. shop.)

Talk About

- What is a pale colour? What is a dark colour?
- Make a collection of crayons, beads, wool, papers, paint shade cards into two groups i.e. pale colours and dark colours.
- Discuss the shades of colour on their clothes, around the room, in paintings by other artists etc.
- Talk about altering a colour by adding more water and making it paler.
- Demonstrate by mixing orange squash - from neat to very diluted!

Doing

- Choose a strip of paper, one primary colour and one paint brush.
- Paint a thin strip of colour down one edge of the strip.
- Use another brush and clean water to paint the rest of the strip making the paint stretch to the other edge. As it gets further from the start it should get paler and paler.
- Talk about what has happened. N.B. Too much paint to start with and the result will be harder to achieve.
- Experiment further with the other two primary colours each on a new strip of paper.

Developing the Idea

- Use circles of paper, put the colour in the centre and drag it to the edges. Turn the paper to avoid leaning on wet paint.
- Use triangles, put the colour in one corner and drag it across the rest. Turn the paper to avoid leaning on wet paint.
- Encourage the children to cut their own shapes of paper, choose where to place colour and where to drag it.

Links with AT2 (Knowledge & Understanding of Other Artists)

Pierre Bonnard

George Seurat

Materials

Paint brushes (thick and thin)
Ready mix paint or powder paint
Palettes/Inking trays
Water pots

Newsprint or Free Art paper 80 gsm
Sugar paper (assorted colours)

Suppliers

NES Arnold Ltd
Ludlow Hill Road
West Bridgeford
NOTTINGHAM
NG2 6HD

Pisces
Westwood Studies
West Avenue
CREWE
Cheshire
CW1 3AD

Philip & Tracey Ltd
North Way
Andover
Hampshire
SP10 5BA

Hope Education
Orb Mill
Huddersfield Road
OLDHAM
Lancashire
OL4 2ST

Yorkshire Purchasing Organisation
41 Industrial Park
WAKEFIELD
WF2 0XE

Printing

Printing

Session   One

Activity   Exploring the technique.
Pressing on and taking off.
Darker and Lighter.

Focus   Shape

Equipment Needed   Ready mix paint - I colour only. Palettes, brushes, paper towels, assorted junk (e.g. bobbins, card, lids, sponge etc.) in trays, background paper A3 or A4 in size, any colour.

Talk About
- The shape and textures of the junk.
- How to hold it and dip in into paint.
- How to print - press on and take off.
- How often to return and add more paint.

Doing
- Print using one piece of junk and one colour of paint.
- Now explore the marks and shapes made with a range of junk.
- Next print by returning to add paint each time.
- Now print with a shape until it runs out of paint.
- Encourage random printing.
- Finally, select and arrange shapes purposefully.

Developing the Idea
- Print with round shapes only - large and small, inside and outside, around the edge etc.
- Rectangles and squares only - large and small, inside and outside, around the edge etc.
- Make a group printing of random shapes.
- Make a group printing of similar shapes.
- Print using different shades of one colour.
- Cut and stuck shapes matched and included with printed shapes.

**Links with AT2
(Knowledge & Understanding of Other Artists)**   Wrapping paper designs.

Printing

Session	Two
Activity	Random Patterns.
Focus	Shape and Pattern.
Equipment Needed	Paint one colour only, circles or squares of white paper e.g. Free Art Paper approximately 15cm by 15cm, strips of sticky paper the same colour family as paint (e.g. a shade of blue), scissors, glue, palettes, assorted junk for printing with, paper towels.

Talk About
- The names of the shapes to be used e.g. squares, circles etc.
- How to arrange and stick paper strips randomly on the white paper
- Where to print the shapes on, off, around the sticky paper strips
- The colour of the paint.

Doing
- Choose a circle or square of white paper and not more than five strips of sticky paper.
- Arrange and stick the strips in any design on the background, next to, across, overlapping etc.
- Now print with junk randomly to enrich the pattern.

Developing the Idea
- Choose a different shape of paper and experiment further.
- Use a different colour of paint for each shape you print.
- Use different coloured strips plus different coloured paint.

Links with AT2 (Knowledge & Understanding of Other Artists)

Patterns in Aboriginal Art

Printing

Session Three

Activity Repeat Patterns.

Focus Colour, Pattern and Shape.

Equipment Needed Assorted junk for printing. Strips of coloured sugar paper about 10cm wide for the background, 2 colours ready mix paint, palettes, brushes, paper towels, counters and beads.

Talk About
- What is a repeat pattern?
- Finding and collecting repeat patterns in the classroom.
- Making repeat patterns using objects such as counters, beads etc.
- Selecting junk shapes for printing a repeat pattern (two only).

Doing
- Choose a strip of paper.
- Use one colour of paint for each piece of junk.
- Print one shape, then the next shape, then the first shape again and so on until you reach the end of the strip.
- Now you have printed a repeating pattern.
- Next try another repeating pattern on a new strip using two different shapes.

Developing the Idea
- Make a repeat pattern in another way on a square of paper.
- Use one shape only for a complete row across the square.
- Now use the second shape for the next row.
- Then use the first shape again and so on until the square is full.
- Finally make a repeat pattern with one shape and two colours by alternating the colours.

Links with AT2 (Knowledge & Understanding of Other Artists) Border patterns on the pages of books, wallpapers and their matching borders.

Printing

Session	Four
Activity	More repeat patterns.

Focus	Colour, Pattern and Shape.

Equipment Needed

Assorted junk for printing with, small pre-cut sticky paper circles, squares, triangles. Strips of coloured sugar paper about 10 cm wide as background. A3 coloured sugar paper, 3 colours of ready mix paint, palettes, brushes, and paper towels.

Talk About

- How we made repeat patterns previously.
- How to arrange cut paper shapes to make a repeat pattern.
- Where and how to add printing e.g. inside, next to etc. to make repeat patterns.
- Demonstrate and allow children to arrange their own.

Doing

- Choose a strip of background paper.
- Choose a number of similar cut paper shapes.
- Arrange and stick them along the strip.
- Add printing - on, inside, next to etc. with one piece of junk on your shapes.
- Choose a second piece of junk and a second colour of paint and repeat print somewhere else on the pattern.
- Finally choose a new strip and make a new repeat pattern on your own.

Developing the Idea

- Make a repeat pattern in another way on an A3 sheet of paper.
- Make repeating rows of the same cut shapes then add junk printing.
- Extend this to alternating rows or alternating shapes (2 only) of cut paper plus junk printing.

Links with AT2 (Knowledge & Understanding of Other Artists)

Patterns on fabrics, wallpaper and wrapping paper.

Printing

Session Five

Activity Experimenting with different surfaces and edges of junk.

Focus Line, Shape and Texture.

Equipment Needed Assorted junk for printing - a small strip of card for each child,1 colour ready mix paint, palettes, brushes, paper towels, A3 and A4 paper as background for the prints.

Talk About
- The different surfaces and edges of I piece of junk.
- The different surfaces on another piece of junk.
- Printing one surface then turning and printing with another surface.
- The different marks and shapes printed.

Doing
- Choose a strip of card.
- Dip one edge in paint and print.
- Now print with another edge.
- Try bending the card strip and printing with it.
- Next fold the card strip and print with it.
- Finally make a pattern with all the different lines you have printed.

Developing the Idea
- Print different lines in one colour.
- Choose another strip of card and another colour and add more lines
- Continue with more colours and more strips of card.
- Print using primary colours only.
- Print the lines observed on e.g. a feather or a twig.

Links with AT2 (Knowledge & Understanding of Other Artists) Patterns on fabrics, wallpaper and wrapping paper.

Printing

Session

Six

Activity

Drawing into print
(monoprinting).

Focus

Line and Shape.

Equipment Needed

Wipeable table top, ready mix paint or water based printing ink, sponge rollers to spread paint or ink on to the surface, A3 or A4 paper on which the print will be pressed, paper towels, palettes to rest rollers on.

Talk About

- How to draw by pressing your finger in paint or ink.
- How to place the paper carefully over the paint or ink.
- How to smooth the paper over the paint or ink.
- How to peel the paper off to discover the print.

Doing

- First roll or sponge the printing ink or paint on to a flat wipeable surface.
- Encourage the children to draw lines and shapes into the ink using fingers, pressing firmly to make strong marks.
- Now place paper on to the drawing and press it down taking care not to move it.
- Next ask them to press the paper down using the palms of their clean hands.
- Finally lift the paper carefully to see the print.

Developing the Idea

- Draw in the paint or ink with other tools, e.g. twigs, feathers, etc.
- Use two colours of ink or paint together for the print.
- Print on different colours of paper.
- Use combs to drag through paint.

Links with AT2 (Knowledge & Understanding of Other Artists)

Wood block and lino prints used to illustrate stories.

Materials

Ready mix paint
Paint brushes (thick and thin)
Palettes/Inking trays
Water based printing ink
Sponge rollers or rubber rollers

Free Art paper 80 gsm or Newsprint
Sticky paper
Sugar paper (assorted colours)
Scissors
Glue
Glue spreaders
Card (4 sheet thickness)

Suppliers

NES Arnold Ltd
Ludlow Hill Road
West Bridgeford
NOTTINGHAM
NG2 6HD

Pisces
Westwood Studies
West Avenue
CREWE
Cheshire
CW1 3AD

Philip & Tracey Ltd
North Way
Andover
Hampshire
SP10 5BA

Hope Education
Orb Mill
Huddersfield Road
OLDHAM
Lancashire
OL4 2ST

Yorkshire Purchasing Organisation
41 Industrial Park
WAKEFIELD
WF2 0XE

Printing

Session 1
Example of printing using round shapes only.

Session 2
Examples of printing using gummed strips as a starting point.

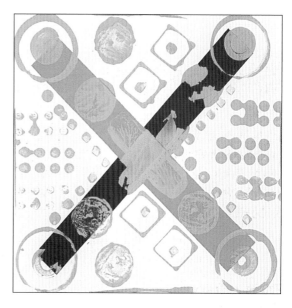

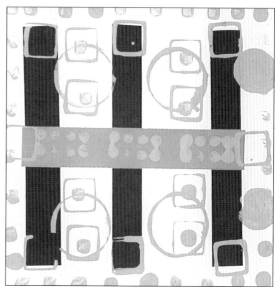

Printing

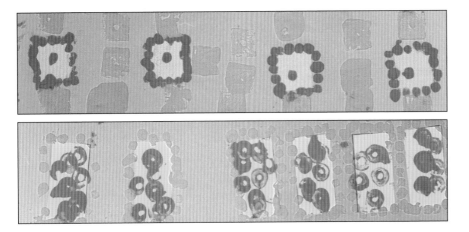

Session 4
Example of printing a repeating pattern starting with cut shapes.

Session 5
Example of printing lines using a strip of card in different ways.

Session 6
Example of mono-printing:- drawing a line in an inked surface and taking a print.

Collage

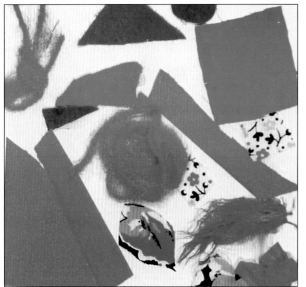

Session 1
Arranging and sticking.

Session 2
Making a group.

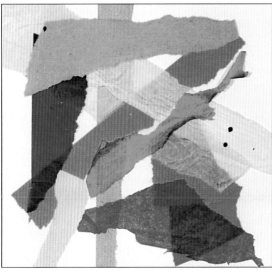

Session 3
Using torn paper strips.

Session 5
Cutting and changing paper strips.

Collage

Our cut and torn, overlapping,
paper collage.

Our cut and torn, fat and thin,
big and little shape collage.

Session 5 & 6
Group work.

Collage

Session   One

Activity   Choosing, arranging and
                      sticking.

Focus   Colour, Shape, Pattern
                      Texture.

Equipment   Scissors, P.V.A. glue, glue spreaders.
Needed   Approximately 10cm x10cm and 15cm x15cm pieces of white or coloured paper as the
                      background. An assortment of coloured card, textiles, tissue paper, foil pieces etc.
                      plus sequins, feathers, ribbons, felt, doilies, etc.

Talk About
- The colours, shapes and textures of the collage material.
- Similarities and differences.
- How to hold scissors and cut safely.
- Where to put the glue and how much to use.
- Sharing resources - not grabbing the lion's share!

Doing
- First choose a piece of background paper either white or coloured.
- Now choose three different things for your collage.
- Lay them on your paper. Move them around until you like the arrangement.
- If you want to change their size or shape do it now.
- This is the stage when you get out the glue and spreaders and ask the children to
  stick their collage material down carefully.
- Finally, the children continue adding, arranging, cutting and sticking until their
  collage is complete.

Developing
the Idea
- Arrange your collage material to make a shape.
- Arrange your collage material to make a pattern.
- Arrange your collage material to make a picture.
- Make a class collage of natural materials collected on a walk.
- Make a class collage of our favourite things e.g. pictures, colours, clothes etc.
  including drawing and writing. Put each child's name on their choice.

Links with   George Braque
AT2
(Knowledge &
Understanding
of Other Artists)

Collage

Session Two

Activity Sorting, classifying and matching.

Focus Colour, Texture and Pattern.

Equipment Needed Scissors, P.V.A. glue and glue spreaders. Trays or boxes for sorting. A collection of textiles, papers, yarns etc. that show similar easily recognised characteristics e.g. textures (rough, smooth, shiny) or patterns (stripes, spots, flowers) or colours (different shades of red, blue, green etc.) Approximately 10cm x10cm or 15cm x15cm pieces of paper, or card (white) as the background.

Talk About
- Possible ways of sorting the materials - establish the idea of a group that is similar in some way.
- Set out e.g. a striped fabric - ask individual children to find other things to join this group.
- Ask one child to set up a group for the class to describe and name.
- Suggest a title for a group, e.g. bumpy, and ask children to find and select materials they think should be in this group.

Doing
- Give the children a square of card on which a piece of material, paper or yarn etc. has been stuck.
- Ask them to look at it carefully, talk about it and describe it. Then add other materials to it by matching what they have seen e.g. colour. When they have made the arrangement, the glue and spreaders can be introduced and the collage stuck down.
- Next ask them to stick one material on a new piece of card and give it to another child to continue and add to, matching it in some way i.e. by colour, pattern etc.
- Finally let the children collect their own group of materials on a third piece of card and talk about why it makes a group.

Developing the Idea
- Make a collage of e.g. the colours I am wearing, the colours in a plant, the colours and shapes in a picture, birthday things, a collage about me etc.

Links with AT2 (Knowledge & Understanding of Other Artists) Story books and wrapping paper illustrated by the technique of collage.

Peter Blake.

Collage

Session   Three

Activity   Torn paper collage.
Tearing paper strips.

Focus   Line Colour and Shape.

Equipment Needed   Tissue paper - assorted colours. A4 size sugar paper - assorted colours. Glue and glue spreaders. 10cm x10cm and 15cm x15cm pieces of white paper for the background.

Talk About
- How to hold paper.
- How to tear paper.
- Tearing long strips and short strips.
- Tearing thick strips and thin strips.
- Where to put the glue to stick the strips down.
- How much glue to use.

Doing
- Choose a piece of tissue paper.
- Tear some long strips - thick and thin.
- Choose a piece of sugar paper.
- Tear some long strips - thick and thin.
- Now get a piece of paper to arrange your long strips on.
- This is the stage when the glue and spreaders are introduced and the children stick their "long strip" collage down carefully.
- Finally repeat the process but this time make a "short strip" collage.

Developing the Idea
- Make a collage of long and short strips.
- Make a collage of strips with spaces between each strip.
- Make a collage where the strips touch, overlap and some are glued on top of others.
- Introduce other papers for tearing and sticking e.g. foil, newspaper etc.

Links with AT2 (Knowledge & Understanding of Other Artists)   Fabric or paper with line patterns e.g. Tartan pattern.

African textiles.

Collage

Session Four

Activity Cut paper collage.
Cutting paper strips.

Focus Line, Shape, Colour, Pattern.

Equipment Needed Scissors. P.V.A. glue and glue spreaders. A4 black sugar paper. White paper A4 as the background - coloured sugar paper A4 size for extension work - A1 for group work.

Talk About
- How to hold scissors
- How to hold paper and cut safely with scissors.
- Long narrow and wide strips.
- Short narrow and wide strips.
- Where to put the glue to stick the strips down.
- How much glue to use.

Doing
- Choose a piece of black sugar paper and a pair of scissors.
- Use your finger to draw a long line on the black paper.
- Now cut a long line using your scissors.
- Cut more long lines.
- Get a piece of white paper to arrange your long lines on.
- Introduce the glue and spreaders and ask the children to stick their "long line" collage down.
- Next ask the children to cut another long line. Talk about changing it into a short line or lines by cutting. Make a "short line" collage by sticking the short lines down on a new piece of paper. Add more short lines to complete the design.

Developing the Idea
- Make a long and short line collage of cut paper strips.
- Introduce a range of colours for cutting.
- Introduce a range of papers for cutting e.g. foil, newspapers etc.
- Make a cut and torn line collage - this could be individual work or a large scale class/group activity.

Links with AT2 (Knowledge & Understanding of Other Artists)

Tartan patterns.

African textiles

Collage

Session	Five
Activity	Cut paper collage. Changing paper strips.
Focus	Line, Shape, Pattern.

Equipment Needed

Scissors, P.V.A. glue and glue spreaders. A4 white paper as the background. A box with an abundance of black sugar paper pre-cut strips 3 x 21cm. and 3 x 10cm. A box of similar strips cut from coloured sugar paper for extension work.

Talk About

- Different lines the children can draw in the air.
- Different lines they can see on their clothes and around them in the room.
- How to hold scissors and draw these lines by cutting in different ways.
- How to hold a strip of paper and where to cut.
- Where to put the glue to stick the strips down.
- How much glue to use.

Doing

- Choose one strip of black paper.
- Use your finger to draw a line that curves or bends along the strip of paper from one end to the other.
- With your scissors now cut a line like the one your drew.
- You should now have two strips of paper - both with curved and straight lines. Save them both.
- Now choose another strip - draw then cut another curved line - make it different from your first one e.g. lots of curves - one big curve and lots of little curves etc.
- At this point introduce the glue and ask the children to stick all their curved lines on their individual pieces of A4. Leave gaps between the strips. Talk about the shapes, lines and spaces.

Developing the Idea

- Explore the same approach but draw, cut and stick zig zag lines.
- Extend to draw, cut and stick lines that change e.g. start with a curve and change to a zig zag.
- Encourage the children to draw, cut, stick and describe new lines of their own.
- Introduce a choice of coloured paper strips for cutting.

Links with AT2 (Knowledge & Understanding of Other Artists)

Henri Matisse

Collage

Session   Six

Activity   Tearing and cutting shapes.

Focus   Shape

Equipment Needed   Scissors, P.V.A. glue and glue spreaders. Wet sand in a tray. A skipping rope. A box of assorted regular and irregular cut and torn shapes. Coloured sugar paper assorted sizes none larger than A4. A3 white paper as background for individual work. A1 white or grey paper as background for group or class work.

Talk About
- Different shapes around them e.g. the shape of bricks, window, buttons, shells, flowers etc.
- Describe the shapes e.g. a spiky shape.
- Draw different shapes with fingers in wet sand.
- Make different shapes with a skipping rope on the floor.
- Choose different shapes of torn and cut paper and describe.

Doing
- Choose a piece of coloured paper.
- Draw a big fat shape on it with your finger.
- Now tear a big fat shape out of the paper.
- Next draw a small, thin shape with your finger.
- Tear a small thin shape out of the paper.
- Try to tear a small, fat shape then a big thin shape.
- Arrange your shapes on A1 or A3 paper (depending on individual or group work).
- Introduce the glue and spreaders and ask the children to stick their shapes down carefully.
- Finally ask the children to tear and add two shapes of their own and describe them.

Developing the Idea
- Extend the same approach but now use scissors to cut out shapes. Stick them down.
- Introduce a choice of colours for both tearing and cutting.
- Create a collage of both torn and cut shapes.
- Create a collage of big shapes with little shapes on top of them - this could be cut or torn or both.

Links with AT2 (Knowledge & Understanding of Other Artists)   Henri Matisse

Materials

Scissors
Glue
Glue Spreaders

Grey sugar paper
Black sugar paper
Free Art paper 80 gsm or Newsprint
Sugar paper (assorted colours)
Tissue paper
Foil
Sequins
Feathers
Ribbons
Doilies
Felt
Textile pieces
Yarns

Suppliers

NES Arnold Ltd
Ludlow Hill Road
West Bridgeford
NOTTINGHAM
NG2 6HD

Pisces
Westwood Studies
West Avenue
CREWE
Cheshire
CW1 3AD

Philip & Tracey Ltd
North Way
Andover
Hampshire
SP10 5BA

Hope Education
Orb Mill
Huddersfield Road
OLDHAM
Lancashire
OL4 2ST

Yorkshire Purchasing Organisation
41 Industrial Park
WAKEFIELD
WF2 0XE

Sculpture

Sculpture

Session	One
Activity	Exploring clay by pulling, pinching, twisting and rolling.
Focus	Shape, Form and Texture.

Equipment Needed

A lump of clay for each child in the group. (Real potters clay is ideal for this activity.) A paper towel or clay board or cloth, for under each piece. A damp sponge in the centre of the table.

Talk About

- What clay is.
- Where clay comes from.
- What clay is used for.
- Make a collection of things made from clay.
- Touch the clay gently - how does it feel? smooth, cold etc.
- Hold it on your hand - how does it feel? heavy, light etc.
- Explore clay using your fingers in different ways.

Doing

- Choose a lump of clay and put it on the paper towel in front of you.
- Roll it under your hand to make a ball.
- Put one hand in the air (not very high) and pull the air with your fingers.
- Now pull the lump of clay in lots of different places in a similar way.
- Next pinch the air with your fingers. Then pinch the clay.
- Now twist your fingers in the air. Then twist the clay.
- Add more pulls, pinches and twists.
- Dampen your fingers on the sponge and gently smooth over the cracks by stroking the clay . Finally talk about the shape you have made.

Developing the Idea

- Find other ways of using your fingers to change a lump of clay.
- Start with a flat piece of clay and change it.
- Try changing a thin piece of clay.
- Change the shape of the clay by working with your eyes closed.

Links with AT2 (Knowledge & Understanding of Other Artists)

Henry Moore.

Sculpture

Session Two

Activity Exploring clay by burrowing, pushing, prodding and poking.

Focus Shape, Form and Texture.

Equipment Needed A lump of clay for each child in the group. (Real potters clay is ideal for this activity.) A paper towel, clay board or cloth for under each piece. A damp sponge in the centre of the table.

Talk About
- What clay is and where it comes from.
- Things made from clay.
- How we used clay before. What our fingers did then.
- Today we are going to explore clay again using our fingers but in a different way.

Doing
- Choose a lump of clay and put it on the paper towel in front of you. Roll it under your hand to make a ball.
- Put one hand in the air (not very high) and burrow one of your fingers in the air.
- Now burrow into your clay with your finger in lots of different places.
- Next push the air with your fingers, then push them into your clay.
- Prod and poke the air, then prod and poke your clay.
- Dampen your fingers on the sponge and gently smooth over the cracks by stroking the clay.
- Finally talk about the shape you have made.

Developing the Idea
- Start with a flat piece of clay and change it using your fingers in the same way.
- Change a lump of clay by both pulling and burrowing.
- Try doing this with your eyes closed.

Links with AT2 (Knowledge & Understanding of Other Artists) Henry Moore.

Sculpture

Session	Three
Activity	Adding pattern and texture to clay.
Focus	Shape, Form, Pattern and Texture.
Equipment Needed	A lump of clay for each child in the group. (Real potters clay is ideal for this activity.) A paper towel, clayboard or cloth for under each piece of clay, rolling pins. A tray of assorted junk to produce texture and pattern e.g. keys, washers, shells, lolly sticks, twigs etc.

Talk About

- Using a rolling pin to flatten the clay.
- The shapes and patterns on the junk.
- Pressing the junk into the clay.
- Smoothing the clay with one finger to rub out a shape or pattern.

Doing

- Choose a lump of clay and put it on a paper towel.
- Roll the clay flat with the rolling pin. Press down as you roll.
- Choose one piece of junk and press it into the clay.
- Lift it out and look at the print you have made.
- Make more prints with the same piece of junk.
- Now try other pieces.
- Finally cover your tile with lots of different prints.

Developing the Idea

- Print a pattern.
- Print a picture.
- Print on a square tile shape.
- Print on a circular tile shape.
- Print on a lump of clay that hasn't been flattened.

Links with AT2 (Knowledge & Understanding of Other Artists)

Actual tiles with impressed patterns. Pots with impressed patterns. Jewellery etc.

Sculpture

Session

Four

Activity

Constructing by cutting, folding and slotting boxes and card

Focus

Shape and Form.

Equipment Needed

Scissors, reclaimed breakfast cereal boxes and cardboard rolls of different shapes and sizes. Short strips and squares of card (about 4 sheet thickness).
The teacher will need to make sure the boxes have at least one end removed.

Talk About

- What is a slit.
- Cutting a line (a slit) in a piece of card.
- Cutting a line (a slit) in a box or tube.
- Slotting a tube, the edge of a box, or a piece of card into a slit.
- How to hold scissors.
- How to cut card firmly and safely.

Doing

- Choose a square piece of card and a pair of scissors.
- Fold the card in half.
- Cut a slit into any edge of your square.
- Slot a strip of card into it.
- Choose a box with one end removed.
- Cut a slit in your box.
- Slot in a strip of card.
- Cut more slits - slot in more cards.
- Try slotting in a cardboard roll or another box.

Developing the Idea

- Fold pieces of card before slotting them into a box.
- Flatten boxes or cardboard rolls, cut pieces out of them to slot into your box sculpture.
- Make a model with 6 things slotted into it.
- Make a model with 3 squares, 2 strips and a box. Slot them together.
- Make a group "slotted" model.

Links with AT2 (Knowledge & Understanding of Other Artists)

Shapes in architecture, sculpture.

Land Art - Andy Goldsworthy and Richard Long.

Sculpture

Session

Five

Activity

Selecting, changing, arranging and joining boxes and card - using glue.

Focus

Shape and Form.

Equipment Needed

Scissors, P.V.A. glue and glue spreader. 15cm x15cm squares of card as the base of the sculpture. Boxes and cardboard rolls of different shapes and sizes. Ready mix or powder paint, brushes, palettes, foil, doilies, sticky paper etc. for decoration.

Talk About

- The different shapes and sizes of the boxes and cardboard rolls.
- How they can stand next to each other and balance on top of each other.
- Changing a box by cutting bits out.
- How to hold scissors to cut firmly and safely.
- Where to put the glue to stick the boxes together.
- How much glue to use.
- How to gently press them together.

Doing

- Choose a box and a square of card.
- Put glue on one surface of your box.
- Press that surface on to your square of card.
- Now choose another box or roll, and stand it next to or on top of your first box.
- Look carefully at where the boxes touch, that is where you need to put the glue. Take the box or roll off now.
- Carefully put the glue on it and put your box or roll back on your sculpture where it was before.
- Finally choose two more boxes and glue them to your sculpture on your own.

Developing the Idea

- Explore making more "glued together" sculptures.
- Cut holes in, remove one or two ends to change shape of some of the boxes you add to your sculpture.
- Use the changed boxes and all the bits you cut off as part of your sculpture.
- Decorate your sculpture by painting it or adding foil, sticky paper,etc.

Links with AT2 (Knowledge & Understanding of Other Artists)

Shapes in architecture.

Sculpture.

Sculpture

Session   Six

Activity   Selecting, changing, arranging and joining boxes and card - using tape.

Focus   Shape and Form.

Equipment Needed   Scissors, brown paper gummed tape, cut into strips. A saucer of water or damp sponge. Boxes and cardboard rolls of different shapes and sizes. Ready mix or powder paint, brushes, palettes, foil, doilies, sticky paper etc. for decoration.

Talk About
- The different surfaces of the tape - the shiny side with gum or, the dull side without.
- How to make the gummed side sticky by dipping it in a saucer of water or on a damp sponge.
- How to stick it on to a box.
- How to stick it across and around two boxes to join them.
- How to gently smooth it down flat.

Doing
- Choose two boxes and stand them next to each other.
- Choose a dry piece of gummed tape.
- Make sure it is long enough to go right round your boxes.
- If it is, then make it sticky by getting it damp on the gummed side and wrap it round your boxes.
- Smooth it down gently.
- Now choose another box - put it next to or on top of your sculpture and look carefully at where the tape must go to join it on.
- Choose your tape and try it for size. Make it sticky and fix the new box on to your sculpture.
- Finally add two more boxes on your own.

Developing the Idea
- Work on making a sculpture with cardboard rolls as well as boxes.
- Use scissors to change the shape of some of the boxes before you use them.
- Cut your own gummed paper strips.
- Decorate your sculpture.
- Make a sculpture using, glue, tape, and slits to join it together.

Links with AT2 (Knowledge & Understanding of Other Artists)   Shapes in architecture.

Sculpture.

Materials

Newclay or Buff School clay or Grey clay
Rolling pins
Scissors
Card (4 sheet thickness)
Glue
Glue spreaders
Readymix or powder paint
Palettes/Inking trays
Foil
Doilies
Sticky paper
Brown paper gummed tape

Suppliers

NES Arnold Ltd
Ludlow Hill Road
West Bridgeford
NOTTINGHAM
NG2 6HD

Pisces
Westwood Studies
West Avenue
CREWE
Cheshire
CW1 3AD

Philip & Tracey Ltd
North Way
Andover
Hampshire
SP10 5BA

Hope Education
Orb Mill
Huddersfield Road
OLDHAM
Lancashire
OL4 2ST

Yorkshire Purchasing Organisation
41 Industrial Park
WAKEFIELD
WF2 0XE

Sculpture

Session 1
Example of changing the shape of clay by pulling.

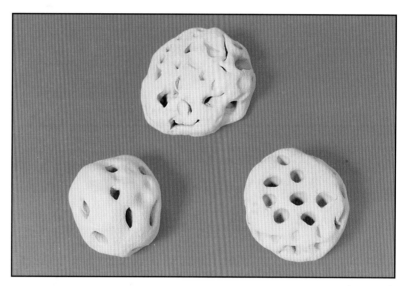

Session 2
Example of changing the shape of clay by prodding.

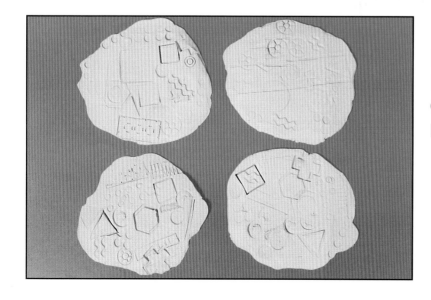

Session 3
Example of adding decoration to clay by pressing.

Sculpture

Session 4
Example of adding to boxes by slotting.

Session 5
Example of joining boxes by gluing .

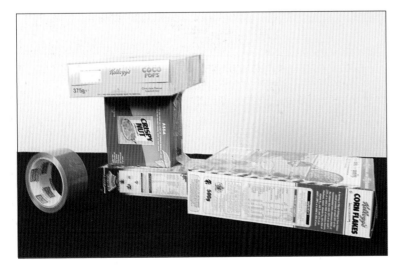

Session 6
Example of joining boxes by taping.

Textiles

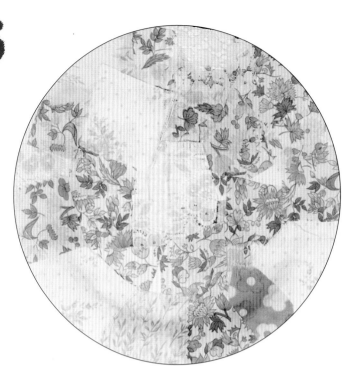

Session 1
Example of choosing, arranging and sticking textiles on a paper plate.

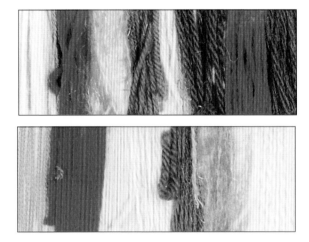

Session 6
Example of wrapping yarns round a piece of card.

Session 2
Examples of joining different textiles using sticky tape and adding decoration.

Textiles

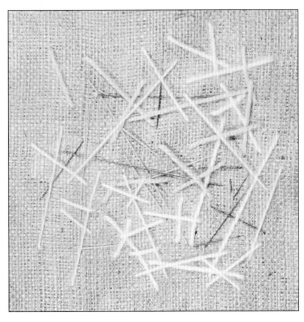

Session 3
Example of sewing using long and short stitches.

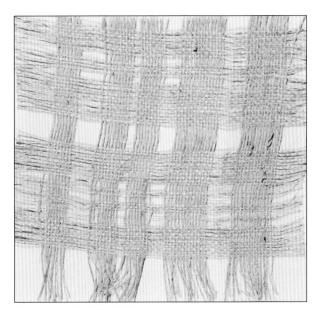

Session 4
Example of unravelling and fraying scrim.

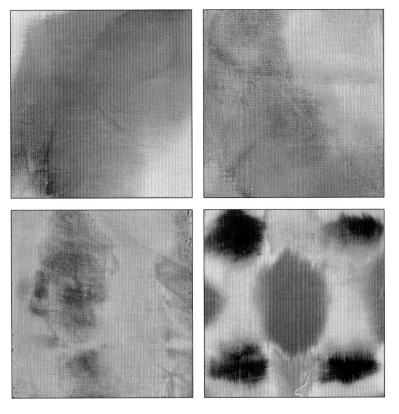

Session 5
Example of dyeing textiles using food colouring.

Textiles

Textiles

Session   One

Activity   Handling and describing textiles. Sorting and matching textiles.

Focus   Colour, Pattern and Texture.

Equipment Needed   A box of assorted textiles e.g. velvet, net, felt, cotton, hessian etc. Cut into small pieces approximately 4cm x 4cm.. Sorting trays, P.E. hoops or empty boxes for the sorted groups of textiles. Paper plates, P.V.A. glue and glue spreaders, sharp scissors.

Talk About
- What textiles are.
- The different textures (furry, shiny, thick etc.) colours (light, dark, bright, red, blue etc.) and patterns (stripes, spots, squares) of the textiles.
- Use P.E. hoops or empty boxes and sort the textiles into groups - each child having a turn. Name each group.
- Encourage them to talk about why their choice joins a particular group.
- Discuss sticking the textiles down - where the glue goes and how much to use.
- How to hold and cut textiles.

Doing
- Choose a paper plate.
- Use a sorting tray to collect the textiles from the group you want to use.
- Talk about your choice.
- Arrange the textiles in the middle of your plate.
- Introduce the glue and spreaders and ask the children to stick their arrangements down one piece at a time.
- Finally use textiles from the same group to go round the edge of the plate.
  Try cutting these into strips or smaller pieces to make them different.

Developing the Idea
- Make an arrangement on a plate of large pieces with small cut pieces on top.
- On another plate choose one group of textiles for the centre and another different group for the edge.
- Make an arrangement of "Textiles I Like" as a collage.
- Make an arrangement of colours and patterns that match those in the classroom.
- Make a patterned and plain arrangement or thick and thin arrangement etc.

Links with AT2
(Knowledge & Understanding of Other Artists)

Michael Brennand Wood

Kaffe Fassett

Textiles

Session   Two

Activity   Cutting and joining textiles using tape and glue.

Focus   Shape

Equipment Needed   Masking tape, assorted textiles cut into a range of shapes and sizes, sharp scissors, P.V.A. glue.

Talk About

- Patchwork patterns that are joined together.
- Textile shapes that will fit together from the group ready cut for them to use.
- Masking tape - how much to undo, how to cut it, where the sticky part is.
- Putting fabric side by side.
- Pressing tape down on two pieces of fabric to join them together.
- Adding shapes on top with glue.
- How much glue and where to use it.

Doing

- Choose two pieces of fabric.
- Put them side by side next to each other.
- Cut a piece of masking tape - to fit the size of the fabric.
- Press it down gently.
- Now choose another piece, put it next to the joined pieces.
- Cut some more tape and join this piece of fabric on. Add one more.
- Finally you have a row of fabric pieces joined together.
- Turn it over and the tape is now out of sight on the back.

Developing the Idea

- Decorate your row of fabric by gluing some smaller shapes on top.
- Cut your own shapes to make a row.
- Add a second row. Decide where else to join and tape.
- Make a square of joined pieces.

Links with AT2 (Knowledge & Understanding of Other Artists)   Patchwork quilt designs.

Textiles

Session	Three
Activity	Sewing textiles and making stitches.
Focus	Line and Pattern
Equipment Needed	Scissors, squares of hessian or scrim (approximately A4 size) - needles with large eyes ready threaded to start with. An assortment of fairly thick threads - pre-cut lengths knotted at one end. A large piece of hessian or scrim for extension/class work.

Talk About

- Using a needle with care.
- How to hold a needle. How to thread a needle.
- How to hold the fabric.
- Making a stitch - in and out of the fabric.
- Long stitches and short stitches.
- Cutting the thread to finish off.
- Putting needles away safely.

Doing

- Try sewing in the air with one finger - in and out - push down then pull through.
- Choose a needle that is already threaded.
- Choose a piece of scrim or hessian.
- Use your needle like your finger - put it under the scrim, point it up, push it through the scrim and gently pull it until the thread stops at the knot.
- Push it down through the scrim somewhere else and then point it up and pull it through.
- Look at the stitch you have made. Now make some more stitches of your own.

Developing the Idea

- Sew only long stitches on your fabric.
- Sew only short stitches on your fabric.
- Sew long and short stitches using lots of different coloured threads.
- Each child make some stitches on a large piece of fabric.

Links with AT2 (Knowledge & Understanding of Other Artists)

Samplers.

Textiles

Session   Four

Activity   Changing the shape of textiles by unravelling, fraying and stretching.

Focus   Texture and Shape.

Equipment Needed   Loose weave textiles that will be easy to fray and unravel e.g. scrim and hessian cut into 20cm x 20cm squares. Textiles that are thin enough to cut into with safety.

Talk About
- The threads that make up the fabric.
- How they fit together.
- Changing the way the threads fit together.
- Pulling threads out.
- Stretching the threads.
- Making a fringe.

Doing
- Choose a piece of scrim and look carefully at the middle of it.
- Put your finger on one thread and follow it right to the edge.
- Now gently pull this thread out.
- Pull out the one next to it.
- Now pull a thread from somewhere else.
- Pull out one thread that is right on the edge.
- Now take out three more next to it. You should have made a fringe.
- Finally poke or push your finger in the middle where the threads are missing. You should have made a hole.

Developing the Idea
- Choose another piece of scrim - make a fringe at each edge and one hole in the middle.
- Choose another piece of scrim. Make two fringes and three holes in a row some large and some small.
- Try out an idea of your own.

Links with AT2 (Knowledge & Understanding of Other Artists)   Baskets - Folk weave type bags that show a woven structure.

Textiles

Session Five

Activity Colouring textiles and adding pattern.

Focus Colour and Pattern.

Equipment Needed Plain white cotton fabric cut into squares approximately 12cm x 12cm. Food colouring (available from most supermarkets) in shallow bowls, a bowl of water, fabric crayons and fabric pens (for extension work), paper towels to lay the fabric on to dry, masking tape.

Talk About
- The colours of the food colouring.
- How to wet the fabric.
- Folding the fabric.
- Holding and dipping the fabric.
- Unfolding the fabric and putting it to dry.

Doing
- Choose a piece of white fabric.
- Dip it in the bowl of water then squeeze it out.
- Now fold your fabric from corner to corner once. Then corner to corner again.
- Dip the first corner in one of the colours.
- Dip another corner in another colour.
- Now hold your fabric along the edge and dip the last corner in another colour.
- Open your fabric, put it on a paper towel to dry.
- Talk about the colours and patterns now on your fabric.

Developing the Idea
- Wet and fold the fabric as before but dip one of the corners in two colours.
- Follow the same steps but fold the fabric differently e.g. in pleats.
- When the fabric is dry and ironed tape it to the table with masking tape and encourage the children to decorate it further by drawing with fabric crayons and fabric pens.
- A hanging can be made by machine sewing the pieces together.

Links with AT2 (Knowledge & Understanding of Other Artists) Textiles showing strong pattern/colours.

Tie and dye examples from Africa.

Textiles

Session Six

Activity Making a textile by wrapping.

Focus Colour, Pattern and Texture.

Equipment Needed Scissors, assorted threads and yarns in pre-cut lengths, strips of card approximately 2.5cm x10cm. Double sided sellotape. Prepare the card by sticking a strip of double sided sellotape on each side.

Talk About
- What the yarn is for.
- What the sticky tape is for.
- How to hold the card and the yarn.
- Where to start.
- How to wrap.
- How to add another colour.

Doing
- Choose a piece of card.
- Hold it in one hand and pretend to wrap some wool round and round it.
- Choose a piece of wool.
- Push one end on to the sticky tape on one side of the card.
- Wrap it round the card making sure it sticks to the tape on the other side.
- Go round again and again until all the wool is used up ending on the sticky tape.
- Now choose another piece of wool and start wrapping again making sure the end is on the sticky tape first.
- Continue wrapping until your card is full.

Developing the Idea
- Wrap with big spaces between the wool.
- Wrap with little spaces between the wool.
- Wrap with no spaces between the wool.
- Use only two colours and make a stripy pattern.
- Use as many colours as you can.

Links with AT2 (Knowledge & Understanding of Other Artists) A collection of striped fabrics, socks, jumpers etc.

Materials

Textile bundles/pieces
Paper plates
Scissors
Glue
Glue spreaders
Masking tape
Scrim
Needles
Hessian
Assorted threads/yarns
White cotton fabric
Fabric crayons/dye sticks
Fabric pens
Double sided sellotape
Card (4 sheet thickness)

Suppliers

NES Arnold Ltd
Ludlow Hill Road
West Bridgeford
NOTTINGHAM
NG2 6HD

Pisces
Westwood Studies
West Avenue
CREWE
Cheshire
CW1 3AD

Philip & Tracey Ltd
North Way
Andover
Hampshire
SP10 5BA

Hope Education
Orb Mill
Huddersfield Road
OLDHAM
Lancashire
OL4 2ST

Yorkshire Purchasing Organisation
41 Industrial Park
WAKEFIELD
WF2 0XE